EXPOSING
SATANIC DEVICES

EXPOSING
SATANIC DEVICES

DOING TARGETED PRAYER WARFARE
VOL. 1

ONYECHI DANIEL

Spiritual Life Outreach, Inc.
Port Harcourt, Nigeria.

authorHOUSE®

AuthorHouse™
1663 Liberty Drive
Bloomington, IN 47403
www.authorhouse.com
Phone: 1-800-839-8640

Published by AuthorHouse   02/11/2013

ISBN: 978-1-4685-0404-0 (sc)
ISBN: 978-1-4685-0405-7 (e)

Unless otherwise noted, all scripture quotations are taken from the New King James Version of the Bible, Copyright © 1990, 1985, 1983 by Thomas Nelson Inc., publisher. Used with permission.

Scripture quotations marked KJV are from the King James Version of the Bible.

Scripture quotations marked NIV are taken from the HOLY BIBLE, NEW INTERNATIONAL VERSION ® Copyright © 1973, 1978, 1984, by International Bible Society.

Scripture quotations marked NLT are from the New Living Translation of the Bible, copyright Zondervan publishers. Used with permission.

". . . lest Satan should take advantage of us; for we are not ignorant of his devices".

—**2 Corinthians 2:11.**

ACKNOWLEDGEMENTS

I had an opportunity to speak in the big mid-year prayer conference of St. Andrew's Anglican Church, Rumuobiokani, Port Harcourt, in 2001. The topic of my teaching was 'Dealing with the prayer environment'. Few days after that conference I was privileged to speak in a Full Gospel Business Men's Fellowship International meeting on 'Dealing with satanic devices'. I acknowledge that the revelations the Holy Spirit gave me while preparing for these two meetings have given rise to the book, *Exposing Satanic Devices.*

I appreciate my wife, Udo Daniel, for her Love, support and prayers while I wrote this book. May I also thank members of my ministration team and others who pray regularly for my literary and other ministries. My gratitude goes to Dr. Steve Ogan for finding time from his busy schedule to edit this work. My thanks also go to Miss Josephine Nna for doing the typesetting, and Pharm. Ike Onyechi for his big support in publishing this book. Thank you and may God reward you adequately.

Onyechi Daniel
June 2003

Contents

INTRODUCTION

Believers in Christ Jesus are in a perpetual state of war. Once you are born again you change loyalty from Satan to Jesus Christ, your new Master. That makes you an enemy of Satan and his wicked kingdom; whether you know it or not. You could become a victim of satanic attacks or devices, if you do not know how to fight back effectively.

Satan has vowed to fight against the Kingdom of Jesus Christ and all who identify with it. This onslaught of Satan is on a continuous basis. No peace talk. No truce. No demilitarized zone. We must accept that Satan is very faithful to his commitment; "to steal to kill and to destroy" (John 10:10a). Satan employs direct and indirect means, and varied devices to achieve his goal.

Believers have been admonished: "resist the devil and he will flee from you" (James 4:7). Believers must know and take full advantage of their new life in Christ, with all the potentials it confers on them, to successfully fight against Satan. They must know their God well, because "the people who know their God shall be strong, and carry out great exploits" (Dan.11: 32b).

However, believers also need to know their enemy—Satan—and his devices. The Bible warns us: "lest Satan should take advantage of us; for we are not ignorant of his devices" (2 Cor.2: 11). What this simply means is that when we are ignorant of satanic devices, Satan will take advantage of us.

The kind of knowledge of Satan and his devices we are advocating here is not that which gives him undue attention or worship. But it is that knowledge that equips us to successfully expose and counter his schemes. Even in modern warfare, a good army would invest time, energy, financial and material resources to study and spy on their enemy to be able to defeat them more easily. The study of an enemy would avoid a very costly victory in terms of human and material losses. This was why the U.S.A. and allied forces invested time and resources to spy on Saddam Hussien and Iraq, before the on-set of the Gulf war in 1991. U.S.A. and the allied forces had sufficient strategic information on Iraq, which helped them to do targeted bombardment of that country, with the war ending in a much shorter time than most people thought. The time, energy and resources invested by the allied forces to spy on Saddam Hussien was not to "honour" or "worship" him, but to be able to defeat him at minimum cost. This s also what the knowledge of the enemy and satanic devices would do for the Church. This is the essence of this book. Let us remind ourselves some scriptural promises that give us advantage in the war against Satan.

"For whatever is born of God overcomes the world. And this is the victory that has overcome the world—our faith. Who is he who overcomes the world, but he who believes that Jesus is the Son of God" (1 John5: 4-5). Please note that 1 John 5:4 says that "whatever is born of God overcomes the world". This is important because it means that marriages, businesses, visions, ministries and other things, not just people alone, that are born of God have the potential to overcome!

"But God . . . raised us up together, and made us to sit together in heavenly places in Christ Jesus" (Eph. 2:4-6). The advantages conferred on the believer in sitting with Jesus in the heavenly places could be glimpsed from Ephesians 1:20-21. God "raised Him from the dead and seated Him at His right hand in heavenly places, far above all principality and power and might and dominion, and every name that is named, not only in this age but also in that which is to come".

"Now thanks be to God who always leads us in triumph in Christ and through us diffuses the fragrance of His Knowledge in every place" (2 Cor.2: 14).

"Behold, I give you the authority to trample on serpents and scorpions, and over all the power of the enemy, and nothing shall by any means hurt you" (Luke 10: 19, emphasis mine).

Yet in all these things we are more than conquerors through Him who loved us" (Rom. 8:37).

"You are of God, little children, and have overcome them, because He who is in you is greater than he who is in the world"(1 John 4:4).

Satan is not a fool. He knows that on a force-to-force basis the believers would easily defeat him because of the enormous advantages of being born of God. He also knows that the scriptural promises only make us potential victors—that there are things we need to know and do to gain the actual victory. So he tries to stop us from knowing and doing what we ought to do to gain victory over him. He also knows that for God's promises to work for us, there are conditions we must fulfill. He therefore tries to keep us from fulfilling the requisite conditions. Satan also knows that though a believer is usually a recipient of God's love and mercy, he can be a recipient of God's wrath if enticed, or pressurized out of the will of God or into sin. So he tries to entice or pressurize us out of the will of God or into sin. Finally, Satan knows that he is not powerless, as a good section of the Church says and sings aloud. He knows that he retained a good part of the power he had as an archangel before he was cast out of heaven to the earth. He encourages the Church to believe he is powerless and harmless—convincing some sections of the church that there is no need to go into spiritual warfare. From the above considerations Satan developed devices to be able to continue to steal, kill and destroy. In employing satanic devices, the enemy's objectives are to attract worship to himself, keep people in captivity, harass, afflict or destroy people and to frustrate God's plan on earth.

For the purposes of this study, satanic devices will include the weapons Satan employs to achieve his goal. Satanic devices include schemes Satan uses to take advantage of the ignorance and/or prayerlessness of believers. They also include wiles Satan uses to entice or pressurize people to sin so that he can establish strongholds to be able to effectively attack a believer whose hedge has been broken. Satanic devices also include Satan's manipulation in which he gets people to offend God so that the wrath of God would fall on them. The bottom line is that satanic devices serve the purposes of Satan and his wicked kingdom. If these devices are not exposed and dealt with appropriately, Satan will have advantage over believers, despite the powerful scriptural promises made to us.

In our prayer warfare we may pray generally against "all satanic devices". But we now know that this kind of "general" prayer does only minimal damage to Satan's kingdom. Our prayer warfare is more effective when we successfully discern the different satanic devices and deal with them specifically. Sometimes God has given us revelations to show that some satanic devices remained standing after we have prayed generally against "all satanic devices". But when we pray against particular devices or weapons of the enemy by name, we see them blown up or consumed by fire, in visions given by God.

It is advantageous for a prayer warrior to know many different satanic devices. In prayer warfare, the Holy Spirit may quicken the believer's mind to deal with a particular satanic device already known by the believer. In this book, therefore, we shall expose different satanic devices from the Bible, from visions given by God and from field experiences. We shall also discuss ways of dealing with these devices taking advantage of revelations on scriptures and/or visions given by God. The principles of prophetic prayers shall be employed in *Exposing Satanic Devices*. (You may please refer to my earlier book: *Waging War With Knowledge*, for a detailed study on the subject of prophetic praying.)

We shall discuss the satanic devices item by item, in a practical way. We shall share testimonies and make illustrations from our field experiences. We shall also give prayer exercises in dealing with the different satanic devices. In reading this book, we join St. Paul to pray that "the eyes of your understanding being enlightened; that you may know what is the hope of His calling . . . and what is the exceeding greatness of His power toward us who believe" (Eph. 1:18-19).

1

PRAYER WARFARE WITHOUT

CHRIST

All over the world there are millions of people who are in churches but who are not Christians. They are encouraged to take part in prayer warfare. Satan is behind this deception.

Some of the so-called churches are not churches at-all. They are actually cults or at best social clubs. 1 Timothy 4: 1-3 throws more light on such groups: "Now the Spirit expressly says that in latter time some will depart from the faith, giving heed to deceiving spirits and doctrines of demons, speaking lies in hypocrisy, having their own conscience seared with a hot iron, forbidding to marry, and commanding to abstain from foods which God created to be received with thanksgiving by those who believe and know the truth".

The fact that Satan is behind these groups is confirmed by the fact that they are "giving heed to deceiving spirits and doctrines of demons" (1 Tim. 4:1). These include religious institutions and groups that impose celibacy (no marriages) for their members or priests. Some forbid their members to eat meat, claiming they are vegetarians. They are the groups who make sacrifices in gardens and burn incense (Isa. 65: 3). Such groups visit burial grounds for strange rituals and are involved in strange 'sanctification' which make them see themselves as 'holy', often keeping some distance from other people (see Isa. 65:4-5). To this group belongs 'spiritual churches', prayer houses and the white and red-garment churches, etc. and all of the eastern religious groups. Many of them go bare-footed on the road or while in their 'churches', under Satan's deception. Some use chaplets, crosses and syanks and holy water and holy oil, etc. The books, constitutions or monographs written by their founders or masters are to them, of higher authority than the Holy Bible, which is Gods word. Many of the groups do not encourage their members to read the Bible for themselves. For some, only their priests could read the Bible and interpret to others. While others pay attention to only a section of the Bible—mainly the Psalms—which they use for prayers.

One common characteristic of people in these groups is that they pray and fast a lot on designated days and hours, with designated number of colored candles or prayer books/materials, or in specified prayer positions. It is strange that these people who are agents of Satan, or at least in the captivity of Satan, are involved in 'prayer warfare' against Satan—sometimes using the name of Jesus. We believe that Satan has to endure their use of the name of Jesus (the one he hates and fears), because the people are serving his purpose in many other ways that we shall see later.

The other group of people who are involved in prayer warfare but without Christ are the unbelievers who are in pentecostal, evangelical or traditional churches. These categories of people have not repented of their sins and have not given their lives to Christ, but they join in prayer warfare when those who have Christ pray. This last group of people remain unbelievers in the midst of believers. The gospel is veiled to them because Satan (god of this world) has blinded their minds to prevent the light of the gospel to shine through to them (see 2 Cor.4: 3-4). Some of them fear what they would loose if they give up their independence to follow Christ.

The truth however is that prayer warfare is not for anybody who is not born again. Only those who are born again are qualified, and are protected in doing prayer warfare against Satan. A person who is not yet a Christian is actually running some risk in engaging himself in prayer against his master Satan. Jesus Christ makes it clear that the Father of the unbeliever is Satan (see John 8:42-44).

Satan encourages these groups and their people to continue in religious pervasion in order to discredit the true church of Jesus Christ. Many people who assume that those people are Christians find enough grounds, from their lives and practices, to criticize the true church. Some people use the confusion offered by these different groups as an excuse to stay away from churches claiming that they do not know the right groups to worship with. While others find enough satisfaction remaining in these perverse groups since they are also called churches and do also pray. Satan also uses them to raise satanic altars to defile the environment so that he can establish strongholds and resist the true church. These people have a form of godliness but deny the power. They are always learning and never able to come to the knowledge of the truth that only Jesus can save (see Acts4: 12).

The way to counter this satanic device is for Christians to pray for the scattering of perverse religious groups. Prayer warfare should be directed against the satanic princes, princesses and demons like the queen of heaven, Eramser spirit, etc., which are behind religious pervasion. The church must pray more vigorously for the souls of all human beings because God "desires all men to be saved and to come to the knowledge of the truth" (1 Tim.2: 4). All Christians should be involved in evangelism and re-evangelization of churches.

Are you saved? Are you born again? Have you given your life to Jesus Christ? Are you truly a Christian? Have you come to the realization of what the Bible says in Acts 4:12: "Nor is there salvation in any other, for there is no other name under heaven given among men by which we must be saved". If you are not yet saved please pray this prayer with all your heart.

"Lord Jesus. I come to you for mercy I realize that I am a sinner, please forgive me. Cleanse me with the blood you shed for me at the cross of Calvary. Please come into my heart and be my Lord and Saviour. I will

4

follow you and live for you all the days of my life. Thank you for saving me, Amen."

Now that you are a Christian you are qualified to be part of the winning army of the Lord Jesus Christ. But please take this scriptural counsel to heart. "You therefore must endure hardship as a good soldier of Jesus Christ. No one engaged in warfare entangles himself with the affairs of this life, that he may please him who enlisted him as a soldier" (2 Tim. 2:3-4).

Prayer exercise

"Father, I rise up against the queen of heaven, Eramser spirit and all demons behind religious pervasion. Come down and sit in the dust O virgin daughter of Babylon. Sit on the ground without a throne—let your throne over these perverse groups be destroyed, in Jesus Name. I uncover your nakedness; let the anger and vengeance of God be released on you in Jesus Name. I set your captives free, and I command your blindfolding over their minds to be broken in Jesus Name. I release the light of the glorious gospel of Jesus Christ to shine into every heart that is not saved, in Jesus name"(Based on Isaiah 47:1-3 & 2 Corinthians 4:3-4).

2

DOCTRINE OF BALAAM

Doctrine of Balaam comes from the story in Numbers 22-25. But its importance as a major satanic device against the church comes from the reference the Lord Jesus Christ made to it in one of the letters to the seven churches. This was in the letter to the church at Pergamos. "But I have a few things against you, because you have there those who hold the doctrine of Balaam, who taught Balak to put a stumbling block before the children of Israel, to eat things sacrificed to idols, and to commit sexual immorality" (Rev.2: 14).

In the story in the book of Numbers, Balak the King of Moab felt threatened by the approach of the people of Israel. He therefore hired Balaam, a powerful prophet, to curse the people of Israel. It must be emphasized that Balaam was so powerful and had built a reputation that when he blessed a person the person was blessed; and when he cursed, the person was cursed. This reputation was summed up in the words of King Balak to Balaam. "I know that he whom you bless is blessed, and he whom you curse is cursed"(Num.22: 6b). That was why Balak was prepared to offer so much so that Balaam would curse Israel.

Balaam could not curse Israel for reasons, which he articulated. The reasons he gave reveal the great advantages we have as children of God. For instance he said in Numbers 23:8; "How shall I curse whom God has not cursed? And how shall I denounce whom the Lord has not denounced?" He also said: "For there is no sorcery against Jacob, nor any divination against Israel" (Num.23: 23a). In other word Balaam was implying that a child of God is invincible to the enemy. However he also implied a condition for this invincibility. "For he has not observed iniquity in Jacob, nor has He seen wickedness in Israel" (Nu.23: 21 a). In other words a child of God is immune to satanic attacks as long as there is no iniquity or wickedness spotted in him or her.

This concept is brought out more clearly in 1 John 5:18. "We know that whoever is born of God does not sin; but he who has been born of God keeps himself, and the wicked one does not touch him." To the extent a child of God keeps himself from sin, to the same extent shall he be invulnerable to Satan's attack. What this means is that it is not totally true to say that one who is born again is immune to attacks of Satan. The complete story is that one who is born again, and stays away from sin, shall be immune to satanic attacks—if he lives up to his responsibility in effective prayer warfare. Sin opens the doorway for satanic attacks. No wonder the Bible says that "who so breaketh an hedge, a serpent shall bite him" (Eccl.10: 8, KJV). Jesus never said or ever implied that Satan was powerless. He once referred to the fact that Satan would find no sin in him as the basis of His confidence. "I will no longer talk much with you, for the ruler of this world is coming, and he has nothing in me" (John 14:30). No serious minded Christian can continue to make the mistake of thinking that Satan is powerless. Who then is behind most sicknesses, accidents, death and destruction? However the power of our Lord and Savior, Jesus Christ, makes nonsense of the power of Satan. Jesus rightly said; "All power is given unto me in heaven and in earth" (Matt.28: 18). We can continue to bask in the power and authority that are in Christ Jesus as long as we stay away from all forms of sin!!

When Balaam could not curse the people of God he gave Balak a counsel (because he was interested in the king's reward), which has continued to work for Satan, till today—that is the doctrine of Balaam. The summary of Balaam's counsel to Balak was that it was a waste of time trying to curse the people of God because they were shielded. But that if the people of God could be enticed or lured into sin then their own God would turn against them. When Israel was so enticed, they fell into sexual immorality with the Moabite women, ate food sacrificed to idols and also bowed to the heathen idols. As a consequence God turned against His own people killing twenty-four thousand of them (Num. 25: 1-9).

Balaam's doctrine gives Satan advantage in two ways. One is that when a believer is enticed to sin he opens a doorway that makes it possible for Satan to successfully attack him. Secondly the wrath of God may be visited upon the believer or church. "For the wrath of God is revealed from heaven against all ungodliness and unrighteousness of men, who suppress the truth in unrighteousness" (Rom.1:18). These two processes can result in sickness, destruction of lives, properties, church-es and institutions. Every unrighteousness is sin. And the so-called "little" or "big" sin could have the above consequences. One sin that all of us are often guilty of is the one described in James 4: 17: "therefore, to him who knows to do good and does not do it, to him it is sin." Another common sin is the sin of anger. Others are those that go against the command of the word of God in Ephesians 4: 29-32. Unfortunately, we can also suffer for sins that we are not aware of. The Bible says "if a person sins and commits any of these things which are forbidden to be done by the commandments of the LORD, though he does not know it, yet he is guilty and shall bear his iniquity" (Lev. 5: 17). In other words, "ignorance of the law is no excuse" as the Nigerian Policeman would often remind you.

How do we deal with this satanic device? We must stay away from all manner of sins including all works of the flesh (see Galatians 5:19-21). When we do sin we must promptly repent before God. "My little children, these things I write to you, that you may not sin. And if anyone sins, we have an Advocate with the Father, Jesus Christ the righteous" (1John 2:1). We must take advantage of the provisions of 1 John 1:8-9 to make ourselves rightagain with God whenever we fall into sin.

When we offend another person we must promptly apologize to the person. Let me say that repenting to God should not be a substitute for apologizing to a person that we have wronged. For some sins, we may not have complete peace, release and victory until we have confessed our faults to the appropriate individual(s).

"Confess your trespasses to one another, and pray for one another, that you may be healed" (Jas. 5: 16a). For some sins, Satan may still find a door open into our life until we do restitution.

Because we may do things that we do not realize are sins before God, it is advisable to do daily repentance of known and unknown sins. We need to pray for ourselves and for other believers, on a daily basis, for God to deliver us from temptation and to give us grace to live through each day without sin. We need to pray for humility and sensitivity to the Holy Spirit to adequately and promptly repent before God when necessary, and to readily apologize to those we offend. We must also do prayer warfare against demons which manipulate us into sin.

Let me mention here that there are three categories of sins that could open doors into our lives to allow for Satan's attacks or God's judgment or both. They are personal, ancestral (or family) and environmental sins. To take care of personal sins we directly repent to God and may need to apologize to the individual(s) concerned. (See Psalm 66:18, 1John 1:5-10). For ancestral sins we repent on our behalf and on the behalf of our ancestors (see Isaiah 65:6-7, Lev. 26:40-42). We may also need to apologize to or make restitution in favour of those (or descendants of those) whom our family (or ancestors) wronged. For sins done in the environment we do identificational repentance—repenting on behalf of those who sinned whether they are dead or alive (see Ezek. 22 : 30-31, Isa. 59 : 1-18, Dan. 9:3-21). It may also be necessary to render apologies or to make restitutions directly or by proxy, as the case may be.

Prayer exercise

"*Father, I truly repent for all the ways I have sinned against you in thought, words and deed; and by failing to do the things that I should do. Forgive me for manifesting the lust of the eyes, lust of the flesh and the pride of life. Lord teach me what I do not see, so that if I have committed iniquity I will commit no more. Deliver me from temptation and please cause me to be more sensitive to the prodding's of the Holy Spirit. Teach me humility and grant me a soft heart that would promptly seek to make amends. Thank you Lord for forgiving me and for restoring me to the place of intimate fellowship with your Holy Spirit, in Jesus name, Amen" (Based on 1John 1: 8-9, Job 34: 32, etc).*

3

SEXUAL IMMORALITY

S exual immorality stands out as one sin with several complications, which serve the purposes of Satan.

The Bible warns: "Flee sexual immorality. Every sin that a man does is outside the body, but he who commits sexual immorality sins against his own body" (I Cor.6: 18). "But now I have written to you not to keep company with anyone named a brother, who is sexually immoral—not even to eat with such a person" (I Cor.5: 11).

These stern warnings, and more, are in the Bible because God knows that sexual immorality brings volumes of trouble, which can affect the present and unborn generations. God says we should resist the devil and he will flee from us (Jas.4: 7). But when it comes to sexual immorality God did not say resist, but flee! Satan has made sexual immorality so pleasurable that it is one of the commonest sins in the world today. There is a massive sex promotion in all aspects of the media. Movies, novels and commercials are hardly complete without a sexual undertone. Young people who have not had the experience of sexual sin are scheming for the opportunity to be initiated. Older people whose strength is failing them are seeking help from drugs, etc., to continue in sexual sins. Unfortunately, sexual immorality is becoming a common sin even in the church.

One of my lecturers in the school of pharmacy reported the result of an experiment done to establish the amount of energy lost per ejaculation in a sexual encounter. Electrodes were placed on the bodies of volunteers to monitor the energy lost during sex. It was reported that the energy lost per ejaculation is equivalent to the energy given by three square meals. This tells us how much of useful energy that could be channeled to productive ventures, which is wasted in indiscriminate sex.

Commenting on sexual sins, the Bible says: "For the lips of an immoral woman drip honey, and her mouth is smoother than oil; but in the end she is bitter as wormwood, sharp as a two-edged sword. Her feet go down to death, her steps lay hold of hell" (Prov.5: 3-5). This scripture suggests one consequence of sexual immorality—a free ticket to hell. Another consequence of sexual immorality is that it leads to loss of honour and wealth. "Remove your way far from her and do not go near the door of her house lest you give your honor to others and your years to the cruel one; lest aliens be filled with your wealth, and your labours go to the house of a foreigner" (Prov.5: 8-10).

Sexual immorality also results in wounds—spiritual, physical and emotional—and enduring reproach. "Whoever commits adultery with a woman lacks understanding; He who does so destroys his own soul. Wound and dishonor he will get, and his reproach will not be wiped away" (Prov.6: 32-33). You will notice that it is so difficult for any servant of God who is implicated in sexual immorality to recover from the reproach—even after many years.

Proverbs 7:6-27 dramatically captures the enticement and stages leading to sexual immorality—but the end is death—Prov.7: 27.

Let us also remind ourselves that God responds to the defilement brought on our body (the temple of God) through sexual immorality with destruction. "Do you not know that you are the temple of God and the Spirit of God dwells in you? If anyone defiles the temple of God, GOD WILL DESTROY HIM. For the temple of God is holy, which temple you are" (I Cor. 3:16-17). This destruction brought about by God, as judgment when the body is defiled, may manifest as sickness, 'accidents', death, etc. That is how seriously God views the matter of defilement through sexual sin or whatever else.

A study of Leviticus 20:10-21 would reveal some other terrible consequences of sexual immorality—especially sexual pervasion. Please notice that these consequences can manifest in a present generation in which the sin was committed or in subsequent generations of those who committed the sexual pervasions. The word of

God says that God may <u>defer</u> or <u>delay</u> the manifestation of his anger to sin. "For my name's sake I will <u>defer</u> my anger . . ." (Isa. 48:9a, emphasis mine). This could result in the consequences of sin manifesting in future generations The immediate or delayed manifestation of God's judgment on sexual pervasion could be death as in Leviticus 20:10-17. It could also, be childlessness as in Leviticus 20:20-21.

From what we have said so far you see why sexual immorality is a very effective satanic device to enslave people and to attract judgment from God. It often leads to sexually transmitted diseases, unwanted pregnancies and abortions, with the complications of bloodshed. Sexual immorality also brings about the transference of some spiritual traits like the curse of poverty, insanity, epilepsy, etc. Sexual immorality implies a covenant, exchange of blood or may even involve a soul-tie. Spiritual transfers through illicit sex would take place with or without the use of condoms!!

One way to deal with this satanic device is to preach the gospel and to enlighten our people concerning the far-reaching implications of sexual immorality. People should be taught to flee sexual immorality and not to try to resist it. We must carry out ruthless warfare against the Queen of heaven (Rev. 17:1-2), Jezebel (Rev.2: 20-21) and water spirits, which encourage sexual sins.

Prayer exercise

"Dear Lord, I bring repentance for my past involvement in sexual immorality—including sexual pervasion. I

renounce every covenant or soul-tie that still keeps me in captivity, in the name of Jesus.

I command the Queen of heaven to come down and sit in the dust. Let her throne be destroyed over my life and environment in Jesus name. I lift up the sword to slay the Jezebel spirit in Jesus name. Let fire consume all you unclean spirits in Jesus name.

I re-dedicate my spirit, soul and body to the Lord Jesus, Amen. "(Based on 1 John 1:8-9, Job.22: 28, Isa.47: 1-3, Rev.2: 20-23, Jer.23: 29).

SPIRIT SPOUSE

The Bible shows that illicit sexual involvement establishes a spiritual marriage. "Or do you not know that he who is joined to a harlot is one body with her? For 'the two' He says, 'shall become one flesh'" (I Cor.6: 16). The New Living Translation of the same passage reads thus: "And don't you know that if a man joins himself to a prostitute, he becomes one body with her? For the scriptures say, '<u>the two are united into one</u>.'" It is therefore clear that sexual relationship outside of marriage establishes a spiritual marriage covenant! It is mainly on this basis that the problems of spirit spouse or sexual intercourse with spirit beings thrive.

Many people have dreams in which they wedded somebody they do not know. Some have dreams in which a particular 'person' lays claim that he or she is married to the victim. Such spirit spouses (spirit husbands or spirit wives, as the case may be) often have sexual intercourse with their victims in the dream. Sometimes unknown faces are involved in the sexual act, but at other times a particular face is the dominant sex partner in the dream. At some other time the face of a person's real husband or wife is used during the sexual encounter. Some ladies experience a situation in which a group of men have sex with them, one after the other. All the varied examples of sex with spirit beings is possible because of an existing sexual/marriage covenant that have not been broken by the victim. Marriage in the spirit realm, or in the rivers, and sexual intercourse with spirit beings serve the purpose of Satan in several ways.

Some people become ill after such sexual encounters in their dream. They are defiled, depressed and discouraged by such encounters. The prayer life of the victims are usually affected, and many of them are no more at their best in any spiritual exercise. For some people the sexual defilement manifests as 'bad luck' or blockade in some areas of their lives. Some fail in examinations, interviews for jobs or in their business pursuits after such sexual ordeals. Others have the chances of marriage blocked by the jealous spirit spouses. Some people have been warned or threatened not to marry anybody in the physical, by their spirit spouses. Some people have been confronted in their dreams for daring to marry in the physical. Some innocent people have had their health, family, finances, etc, attacked because they married somebody who has a spirit spouse. Some women are not able to have children after marriage following the hindrances set-up by their spirit husband or spirit children. Women who have spirit children have sometimes seen themselves give birth to children in the dream, when they are not able to conceive in the physical. Some ignorant women have even prayed to 'claim' such spirit babies born in their dreams, thinking that God was showing them the babies He was giving them. Some people who have spirit spouses find it difficult to enjoy a normal love life with their physical partners.

One common experience is that the sexual dreams persist even after the victims have fasted and prayed—sometimes even after undergoing some deliverance. Some cases that came to us reported that they still had the sexual attacks at the end of three days fasting and prayers—at the very last night of their fasting and prayers! Some others reported that the sexual ordeal increased from one to three a night, after prayer/fasting. I know a particular sister who was warned by her spirit husband not to ever get married. That made her reject many proposals for marriage from many Christians and even pastors. Eventually she decided to accept the marriage proposal from a particular Christian brother. She was struck with a particular strange affliction, which eventually led to her death before the marriage could take place.

For certain people, some satanic rites and ministrations gave them over in marriage to spirit spouses. Such ministrations include those made in prayer houses and in native doctor's homes. They include ministrations that involve throwing sacrifices into the rivers or being subjected to 'spiritual baths' by satanic priests in riversides or from buckets of water from the stream, etc.

For some others, their parents knowingly or unknowingly gave them over in marriage to spirits before they were conceived, while they were in the womb or while they were babies or children. Such babies were sold to Satan while their parents sought occult powers, the fruit of the womb or some other favors from deities. Satan of course would lay claim to such children in the early or later parts of their lives. Other people gave themselves over to spirits for marriage, knowingly or unknowingly, while taking part in traditional dances, masquerade displays, cloth-tying ceremonies, manhood or womanhood initiation rites, and during other initiations into cults.

All of these illustrations are not to show that Satan is more powerful than God, but that God's people could suffer or even be destroyed for lack of knowledge (see Hosea 4:6 and Isaiah 5:13). Prayer/fasting and deliverance ministrations following the problems of spirit spouses could fail, if the nature of the covenant is not understood and dealt with appropriately. Some people have had themselves entangled the more because they sought help, in frustration, from the wrong places. The first step in deliverance from spirit spouse for a person not born again is to lead such a person to Christ. Such a person will not receive lasting help unless he or she completely surrenders to the Lord Jesus. Some people have sought deliverance from the menace of spirit spouses without a readiness to give their lives to Jesus. This will not work (see Colossians 1:12-14). A believer who has a spirit spouse problem should confess of known sins that opened the door-way to Satan, and rededicate one's life to Jesus.

22

The next step is to probe into the past of one's life or even parents' life, to establish how the spiritual marriage covenant was established. The commonest route is sexual immorality. One day or a few days of prayer/ fasting with repentance for sexual sins often opens the door of deliverance. Others we ministered to were helped only after we led them to do specific repentance for sex with partners they could mention by name, followed by the renunciation of the spiritual marriage covenant established in each case. Similarly, specific repentance, with fasting, should be done over satanic rites or ministrations which many have established spiritual marriage covenants. Such marriage covenants should be revoked violently. It will help to get the parents who gave their children over to such marriages to revoke the spiritual transactions, when applicable.

The deliverance ministrations for such victims may be concluded by praying over the victim, anointing him or her with oil, to cancel the marriage contract. It often helps to destroy the invisible spiritual wedding ring by anointing the fourth finger of the left hand with oil. Prayer warfare should be done to destroy the invisible marriage certificate and all the tokens or gifts, given or received, to establish the spiritual marriage.

Prayer exercise

"Father, I sincerely repent of every involvement in sexual immorality. I repent for involvement in any satanic rite or ritual that has given me over in marriage to any spirit being. I renounce such marriages in Jesus name. I declare that I have been bought over by the blood of

Jesus. I set on fire any existing marriage certificate or tokens/gifts associated with this marriage. I lift up the sword and slay all spirit children born in this illicit marriage in Jesus name.

I sanctify myself afresh—spirit, soul and body—with the blood of Jesus." (Based on I John1: 8-9, I Peter 1:18-19, I Cor.6: 19-20, 2 Cor.7: 1).

5

ILLEGITIMATE CHILDREN

One of the consequences of sexual immorality is the raising of illegitimate children—children born out of wedlock. However we must make it clear that for the purposes of this discussion, illegitimate children include children conceived out of wedlock. Such children may have been "socially" protected because their parents wedded before they were born—their mothers being pregnant on the wedding day. The spiritual complications around illegitimate children and their mothers serve the purposes of Satan.

Illegitimate children are usually the most troublesome and destructive in the family. They are usually more rebellious than the average children, often running away from home. Many people's experience is that attempts to help them are often frustrated. Illegitimate children are involved in social vices like smoking, drinking, sexual immorality, stealing, gambling, etc—more than the other children. Often times they end up also having illegitimate children. They do not become Christians easily and when they eventually become Christians, many are on and off in their Christian commitment.

In many cultures illegitimate children are accepted, with full legal rights like other children. While this may have a social merit it is one of the schemes of Satan to continue to encourage the breeding of illegitimate children. In the past, some social stigmas acted as deterrent to the breeding of illegitimate children.

The problems of illegitimate children are basically spiritual. The Bible says that it is by the Lord's mercies that we are not consumed (Lamentations 3:22). The major problem of illegitimate children is that there is a curse on them, which denies them of the mercies of God. "I will not have mercy on her children, for they are the children of harlotry" (Hos.2: 4). Illegitimate children do not experience the fullness of God's love. New living translation of Hosea 2:4-5 makes things very clear. "And I will not love her children as I would my own because they are not my children! They were conceived in adultery. For their mother is a shameless prostitute and became pregnant in a shameful way. She said, 'I'll run after other lovers and sell myself to them for food and drink, clothing of wool and linen, and for olive oil"

This curse on illegitimate children can be broken through prayer ministrations. The first step is to do deep-seated repentance for the sexual immorality that led to their conception and birth. They can pray for themselves in fasting, or an anointed servant of God could pray for them for the curse to be lifted. Prayers should be said for the love and mercies of God to be restored on them. Then, all the spirits that took advantage of the anger of God against them to oppress them should be bound and cast out.

Prayer exercise 1

"Father, I bring repentance on behalf of my biological parents, for the sexual immorality that led to my conception and birth. I ask for your mercy over my life. Please accept me as your child. Jesus has become a curse for me by hanging on a tree; so let every curse over my life be lifted in Jesus name.

Lord cause me to be a beneficiary of your love and mercy in Jesus name, Amen." (Based on I John1: 1-2, Hos.2: 4-5, Gal.3: 13)

In concluding this section, we must mention that the Bible shows that a woman who has bred an illegitimate child is also under a curse from God. If the woman is still continuing in adultery the curse of Hosea 2:3 may take a toll on her. In that scripture the curses pronounced by God include:

"I will strip her naked".

"I will make her like a wilderness and set her like a dry land".

"I will slay her with thirst".

The manifestations of these curses bring a lot of problems in the lives of way-ward women. The summary of what ladies seek from men for which they are enticed into sexual immorality is shown in Hosea 2:5. They include food, drink, clothing and oil (Cosmetics). Yet they will not be satisfied because of the curse from God in Hosea 2:3.

God's curse spoken of in Hosea 2:6 can still affect even a Christian woman who has stopped adulterous relationships, but who has raised an illegitimate child previously. The bible says:

"For their mother has played the harlot . . . . Therefore, behold I will hedge up your way with thorns and wall her in, so that she cannot find her paths" (Hos.2: 5-6). Unless a woman who has raised an illegitimate child is ministered to she may find a lot of hindrances ("thorns") and blockades ("wall her in") in her experiences. This curse may affect her marriage, ministry, career, finances, etc.

Prayer exercise 2

"Father, I bring repentance for the fact that I had raised an illegitimate child. I completely repent of, and renounce adultery, in Jesus name. I ask that you have mercy on me. Please remove the thorns and the blocking walls out of my way, in Jesus name. Kindly show mercy on the child I had out of wedlock in Jesus mighty name". (Based on 1 John 2:1-2, Hos.2: 3-6, John 14:13).

ACCUSATION MINISTRY

OF SATAN

Satan is the accuser of Christians. Satan was referred to in Revelation 12: 10 as the one "who accused them before our God day and night." Satan's interest in the word of God is not so that he will obey them and live by them. It is so that he will know when Christians have not lived up to the standards of the word of God so he can level accusations against them before God. However we must bear in mind that Satan does not try to accuse us falsely before God. He knows he will never be able to deceive God. He successfully accuses us when there is a justification for it.

Through this wicked ministry Satan is able to dig out our sins, failures or things in our foundation to accuse us with. Christians need to bear in mind that Satan is able to accuse us based on things in our personal, ancestral or environmental foundations. (My book, *Faulty Spiritual Foundations* will address this more adequately. See also the chapters on Spiritual Mapping in my book; *Waging War With Knowledge)*. Be reminded that the Bible says: "If the foundations are destroyed, what can the righteous do" (Ps. 11: 3). In other words, our righteousness cannot carry us over a faulty foundation. We are robbed of part of our benefits for being righteous, if Satan can discover the faulty foundations upon which he will accuse us before God.

The way this accusation ministry of Satan goes on is for him to present his argument against us, say like this; "The righteous one, this daughter of yours has been asking you for the fruit of the womb. She should not get it, and I must be allowed to destroy the baby in her womb because she has killed babies through abortion." In the above example, Satan may base his submission on Numbers 35:33 in which the scripture says that the blood of one who has shed blood should be shed. His accusation may also be based on the continuous cry of the shed blood; "O earth do not cover my blood, and let my cry have no resting place" (Job 16: 18).

A sister we once ministered deliverance to came back to share a dream she had with me. In that revelation she was made to see two men. One was digging frantically as if looking for something. The other man began to dissuade him saying that the sister in question had made effort to deal with things in her life, requesting the first man to let her go. But this man insisted that he wanted to dig some more to discover what he would still use against that sister. That revelation taught us that the enemy does not only try to uncover 'incriminating evidence' but that when we successfully deal with some things in our life, he will still be digging for fresh evidence. We must say here that when we fail to deal with our evil foundation, our foundation will deal with us. The Bible shows clearly that the way to get free from the consequence of any sin, no matter how long ago it was committed, is to confess it so that it could be remitted. "He who covers his sins will not prosper, but whoever confesses and forsakes them will have mercy" (Prov. 28: 13).

Unfortunately, Satan sometimes delegates this accusation ministry to believers who become critical, judge and accuse other believers mercilessly. Such believers or ministers become co-workers with Satan to tear down the church or other believers/ministers. In discussing the kind of fast acceptable to God, and the conditions for receiving an answer from God (Isaiah 58: 9a), the Bible says: "If you take away the yoke from your midst, the pointing of the finger, and speaking wickedness . . ." (Isa. 58: 9b). The "pointing of the finger" is Satan's accusation ministry done through a willing vessel—it introduces a yoke in the midst of the brethren! The Bible is full of proper ways of dealing with wrong and making corrections—for instance see Mathew 18: 15-17. The Bible also clearly says; "Brethren, if a man is overtaken in any trespass, you who are more spiritual restore such a one in a spirit of gentleness, considering yourself lest you also be tempted" (Gal. 6: 1). Whenever we go beyond the provisions of scripture we will be helping Satan to steal, kill and destroy—whether we know it or not!!

Prayer exercise

"Father, I confess all known and unknown sins in my life. I also repent for every sin my parents and ancestors have done against you. I bring before you all the sins done on this land/house by past and present occupants. Father please forgive and wash them away with the blood of Jesus. I also repent for any ways I have joined Satan to accuse the brethren. Lord forgive me and please touch the hearts of those affected to forgive me. I now condemn every tongue that rises against me in judgment, in Jesus name. Let such tongues be still forever, in Jesus mighty name" (Based on Lev. 26: 40-42, Lev. 18: 24-25, Ezek. 22: 30-31, Isa. 54: 17b).

The other part of Satan's accusation ministry is that he also accuses God before the brethren. Satan is very eager to 'prove' to us that God does not love us, that He is unfaithful, that His word is not true and that He does not answer prayers. When we go through trials and wilderness experiences that would work out God's purpose and things for our own good (see 1 Peter 5:10), Satan would tell us that we are suffering because God does not love us. When we pray and hold onto the word of God and nothing seems to happen, Satan would rush in to accuse God of unfaithfulness before us. Many people have fallen to this ploy of Satan; being angry or bitter against God. Some have given Him rude ultimatums to act immediately or loose them. If we understand what the scripture says about God, we will never allow ourselves to be deceived enough to be angry or bitter against God. "He is the Rock, His work is perfect; for all His ways are justice, a God of truth and without injustice; righteous and upright is He" (Deut. 32:4). Every believer or minister must go through experience(s) of trials, pains and confusion one time or the other. But when you do the right things, wait and continue to love and trust God, things would become clearer.

Prayer exercise 2

"Dear Lord, I am sorry for the times I felt that you have failed me. I am sorry for my anger and bitterness against you. I now know that you can never do wrong. I know that the thoughts you have for me are the thoughts of good and not of evil. I pledge my love for you forever no matter the situation I find myself.

Arise O Lord on my behalf and let your enemies be scattered in Jesus name, Amen" (Based on Deut. 32: 4, Jer. 29: 11, Ps. 68: 1).

7

CLOUD OF TRANSGRESSION

Satan may entice or pressurize individuals, families or communities to pile up sin upon sin. The result is that a cloud of transgression forms over the territory where the iniquities are committed. Such a cloud of transgression would shut off both the light and rain of God's blessings from getting through to the people in that territory. Even creation may be hindered by such a cloud. A righteous man who comes into that territory could be affected adversely. So could churches, businesses or projects established by righteous people in that territory be affected. It will be very difficult, if not impossible, to experience God's blessings and breakthrough in an area covered by clouds of transgression. It will also be difficult for one to get one's prayers through to heaven, or get answers to prayers under such situations. God has sometimes revealed such clouds of transgression over some families or communities where my team and I have gone for family, community or territorial deliverance assignments.

The way out is to intercede for the people or area and to encourage repentance amongst them so that God may blot out the cloud of transgressions. "I have blotted out like a thick cloud, your transgressions, and like a cloud your sins. Return to me, for I have redeemed you". (Isa.44: 22).

Pleading the blood of Jesus into the atmosphere would also help to break up the cloud of transgressions. The whole environment could then be reconciled to God by the blood of Jesus (see Colossians 1:20).

Prayer exercise

"Father, I bring repentance over the sins of these people and the sins committed in this environment. I ask, dear Lord, that you may please blot out the cloud of transgressions that is a barrier between this land and you. I purge the oppressive atmosphere by the blood of Jesus. I reconcile this whole territory back to you in Jesus name, Amen". (Based on Isa. 44:22 and Col. 1:20).

When God answers it is like the whole creation comes alive and breaks forth into singing. It shall be like a springtime experience—breakthrough and restoration shall follow. It is this scenario that Isaiah 44: 23 captures in a poetic form:

"Sing, O heavens for the LORD has done it! Shout, you lower parts of the earth; Break forth into singing, you mountains, O forest, and every tree in it! For the Lord has redeemed Jacob, and glorified Himself in Israel."

VEIL OF DARKNESS

Veil of darkness works in a similar way to a cloud of transgression. Again, God has revealed this canopy-like covering over many families or communities. Sometimes, as God has revealed, iniquity is responsible for the formation of the veil of darkness. Sometimes, God had revealed to us what particular iniquity or iniquities that are implicated.

Sometimes, however, the veil of darkness comes as a result of satanic programming from witches, wizards or other satanic agents. This is confirmed by the scripture of Isaiah 30:1, KJV.

"Woe to the rebellious children saith the LORD, that take counsel, but not of me; <u>that cover with a covering,</u> but not of my spirit, that they may add sin to sin" (emphasis mine).

The way to deal with this satanic device would depend on whether it was formed due to sin or due to satanic programming. We must accept, however, that sometimes a person to whom God has given a revelation of a veil of darkness may not know its origin. In that case it may be wise to first bring repentance and deal with it as if it came because of iniquity—just as we have discussed under the 'cloud of transgression'. Sometimes, a person may not have been given the vision of a veil of darkness but may sense its existence considering his experiences or observations in a particular territory. In that case such a person should go on and deal with the veil of darkness. Isaiah 25: 7 is a scripture that can be used in prophetic prayers to deal with a covering veil of darkness. "And He (God) will destroy on this mountain the surface of the covering cast over all people, and the veil that is spread over all nations."

Prayer exercise

"Dear Lord I bring repentance for every sin and iniquity responsible for this covering cast over this territory. I ask that you may please blot out this covering of darkness over the land in Jesus mighty name.

Your word says that upon this prayer mountain you shall destroy the surface of the covering cast and the veil of darkness over the people. I ask that you please go ahead and destroy them in the name of Jesus. Let your anger and judgment be visited on the children of rebellion who are responsible for this satanic covering if they fail to repent, in Jesus mighty name, Amen". (Based on Isa. 44:22, 25: 7, 30:1).

NOISE OF ALIENS/SPIRITUAL NOISE

This noise of aliens can be in the spiritual or physical realms. One may sometimes notice that it is difficult to settle down to pray, meditate or engage in any worthwhile spiritual exercise in some environments. This spiritual 'noise' may continue to be a nuisance to a Christian who comes into a new territory, before he is able to 'tame' that territory. Such noise may be 'heard' in the spiritual, without any physical manifestation, especially when one wants to pray or read the Bible. Sometimes no actual noise is 'heard' in the spiritual, except that there is an unsettling effect in the atmosphere that robs one of concentration to pray or study the Bible, etc. Sometimes it is not easy to put words to the experience, except that one can do all other things easily in the environment, except spiritual exercises.

In one compound we ministered family deliverance in Delta State, members of the family used to hear the cry of a baby outside around midnight. When they went outside they did not see any physical baby crying. The

Lord revealed to us that the noise was the protest of a baby killed in cold blood in the past. That cry was more like the cry written in Job 16:18. "O earth, do not cover my blood, and let my cry have no resting place!" However after we brought identificational repentance for the bloodshed done (may be by abortion, child sacrifice, etc.) we were able to silence that noise in the environment.

In some cases, spiritual or physical noise in an environment could be satanic protest. The spiritual or physical noise may be like a persistent humming sound or satanic protest in the form of animal noise, e.g. like giant rats or giant footsteps on the roof or ceiling during midnight hours. It may also take the form of satanic singing and/or drumming in the environment. It may take the form of the voice of Satan speaking to a person to intimidate or cause fear—almost like the experience people who are suffering from schizophrenia have. We have ministered to people who always heard taunting and harassing voices. We have once gone on a prophetic action to the house of a man of God to do prophetic action; part of which was to stop the spiritual satanic drumming and dancing that went on at the back of the man's house. (See the case study: 'Spirit of giant-killer stopped' in my book *Waging War with Knowledge* for details).

When my family and I moved into a new area of Port Harcourt there was a lot of protest noise in the environment because of the levels and depths of prayer my team and I began to do in the new place. It also brought us some counter attacks engineered by one occult man, who was operating a 'Sabbath Church', and who held sway in the environment before we came. God expects us to deal with the noise of aliens. "You will reduce the noise of aliens, as heat in a dry place; as heat in a shadow of a cloud, the song of the terrible ones will be diminished" (Isa. 25:5). In dealing with the noise of aliens we may need to start with identificational repentance for the sins that gave Satan undue right in the place or which implies a dedication to Satan. We can then silence the noise—whether manifesting in the physical or spiritual—by the blood of Jesus, insisting that the blood of Jesus should speak better things for us. We may also pray by the scriptures in Psalm 29:3-9, using the voice of the Lord to silence all other voices.

Prayer exercise

"Father, I bring repentance for any sins committed here that have given Satan right to exercise dominion over this place. I reconcile this environment to God by the blood of Jesus. I demand that the blood of Jesus should silence every speakings and satanic noise in this environment in Jesus name. Let the blood of Jesus speak peace and quietness in Jesus name.

I bring the voice of the Lord against the noise of aliens in Jesus name. The God of glory thunders, the voice of the Lord is powerful, the voice of the Lord breaks the cedars of Lebanon, so let the voice of the Lord forever silence the noise of aliens and all spiritual noise in Jesus mighty name". (Based on Col. 1:20, Heb. 12: 24 and Psalm 29: 3-9).

10

SATANIC TOKENS AND TOTEMS

Tokens and totems are instruments of satanic claim. They may also be seen as spiritual instruments released to guarantee a coming satanic manifestation.

While totems may be animal parts or whole animals like tortoise, lizards, chicken, dog, goat, ram or cow, etc; tokens are varied materials like coins, red or white cloth, staff of office (like 'ofor' in Igbo language), coloured candles, cowries, newly formed blade of palm tree (called 'omu' in Igbo language), etc.

Sometimes God gives people revelations of these tokens or totems as the things behind their problems. The presence of these totems or tokens in the physical or spiritual opens up a place to satanic oppression. Native doctors, diviners or false prophets would usually ask for these totems or tokens for their satanic ministrations. Their ministrations often involve the sacrificing or burying of these tokens and totems in key places in a compound—like the gate, forecourt of a compound or inside the sitting room or bedroom.

Their presence makes for ease of demonic traffic. Often times the release of a token in the spiritual realm precedes a satanic attack or disaster.

In one case a couple's religious practices, as eckists were not sufficient to protect them from armed robbers who were pillaging their environment. They allowed a native doctor to bury the head of a ram, etc, at their gate for protection against robbers. After that there were all sorts of problems in their home and the couple's marriage of over thirty years was badly threatened until God used us to intervene.

To deal with tokens and totems, we first of all need discernment to recognize them for what they are—even when they are presented in modified or 'civilized' forms. We should repent for their existence and go on to destroy them and burn them with fire (see Deut. 12:1-3).

If the tokens or totems have been buried in the ground they could be dealt with in two major ways. One way is to dig them up and burn them with fire when their positions are known and are still accessible (see Deut. 7: 5); if the Holy Spirit leads that way. Satan would desire to use them as door-openers into people's lives and premises no matter how long ago they were buried. But sometimes God may reveal these tokens and totems in the spiritual realm, in dreams and visions. They could be destroyed employing the scripture of Isaiah 44:25.

Prayer exercise 1

"Father I repent for the existence of satanic tokens and totems in this environment. Open my eyes to be able to spot satanic tokens and totems for destruction in Jesus name.

Lord, you frustrate the tokens of liars and drive diviners mad. May you frustrate every satanic token and totem and burn them with your fire in Jesus name. If the diviners who employ them do not repent, drive them mad according to your word in Jesus name. I use the token of the blood of Jesus to counter the effect of every satanic token in Jesus name". (Based on Isa. 44: 25 & Rev. 12:11a)

Another way to deal with tokens/totems is to do prophetic prayers in which you command the earth to devour or swallow the tokens / totems; or to vomit them so that the fire of the Holy Spirit can devour them. This approach could be used to deal with tokens/totems that are no more physically accessible—say those under the foundation of buildings—or when the Holy Spirit does not lead you to begin to dig up accessible ones, which may be too many.

Let us share this testimony that illustrates the long term damage a token could do, how God could give help towards discerning the token implicated and what length one could go to deal with such tokens. After hearing some of our teachings on dealing with faulty foundations a pastor approached us for counselling and deliverance. At that time he was experiencing a series

45

of problems and difficulties with his relations, finances and ministry. He told me that the church assembly he started eight years before has just closed down and that all the members were scattered. He said that in the past, that the church would close down and all the members scatter after every two years. He said that after every scattering he would relocate and start to build up a new congregation only for the same fate to befall his ministry—yet he was a full—time pastor.

In the process of the preparation to move in with my team to minister to him and his family, I asked him to write his spiritual history (or spiritual mapping) guided by the format my ministry normally uses. One of the things he wrote down was that his parents had cause to take him to a river when he was a baby, on the recommendation of a native doctor, who accompanied them for a satanic ministration. The conclusion of that ministration was that coins were thrown into the bottom of the river before his parents took home the baby. I would have missed the significance of the token thrown into the bottom of a river if not for the help of the Holy Spirit. While my team and I were interceding for this man of God and his family, before the family ministrations, the Lord revealed to us that what was holding His servant was at the bottom of a river. It was after this ministration that the Holy Spirit led me to read the pastor's spiritual mapping and my eyes and understanding were quickened to the matter of the token of coins in the bottom of a river. The only problem was that the coin was cast into a river in another state where the parents of the pastor were residing then, and that was more than forty-five years ago. The pastor has not been in that town again since he left there as a child more than forty years before. We were all excited at these revelations, yet Satan fought and delayed our trip to this river for almost two years.

Eventually we went last year. We drove through terrible roads (with a driver, the pastor, my assistant and I) to locate that remote village. When we could not go any further in the car we parked it, and went some distance on foot to locate the river. The Holy Spirit helped the pastor to correctly identify the river, after asking the villagers for directions. When the pastor, my assistant and I got to the river, I said an opening prayer. In that prayer I thanked the Lord for the trip formally telling Him why we were there. Then I also addressed the goddess of the river, making it clear that the man with me is a servant of God whose destiny she has delayed for about 48 years and that we have come to undo what was done in 1953. Then I asked the pastor to bring repentance before God for what was done in the past, etc. After this I went on to minister cancellation of the evil dedication, separating him and his destiny from the coin in the bottom of the river and the mystery of the water kingdom before praying for the destruction of the token. After that, I anointed the pastor with oil by that same river and proclaimed his freedom by the authority in the name of Jesus Christ. The pastor's life has never remained the same again, as he spoke to me few months later—praise God!!! Since that ministration, the pastor has had many testimonies as he reported.

Prayer exercise 2

"I bring repentance to God for every token/totem that have been buried in this land. With the blood of Jesus Christ I silence your speakings in Jesus name. Only the blood of Jesus, which speaks better things, will speak on this land henceforth. I release the fire of the Holy Ghost to burn all seen and unseen tokens/totems in Jesus name. I command you land to eat up and swallow all tokens/totems buried in you in Jesus name" (Based on 1 John 1:8-9, Heb. 12:24, Num. 16:30-31).

11

MYSTERY OF MASCOTS AND

SYMBOLS

The Longman Family Dictionary definitions of the two key words above would help our discussion.

MASCOT: "A person, animal, or object adopted as a (good luck) symbol".

SYMBOL: "Something that stands for or suggests something else by reason of association, convention, etc".

Mascots or symbols which have demonic backgrounds, are satanic devices that are often over-looked by prayer warriors or intercessors. The existence of such mascots or symbols in a room, house, church, industry, military regiment or a place gives Satan undue right into the place or into the lives of the people there. The existences of such things are signs of dedication to Satan. Satan will not hesitate to lay claim to anything, place or persons knowingly or unknowingly dedicated to him. Such mascots or symbols are known to open up a place or a person's life to demonic traffic.

Notice that King Josiah did not spare mascots in the reformation he carried out in Israel. "Then he removed the horses that the Kings of Judah had dedicated to the sun, at the entrance to the house of the LORD, by the chamber of Nathan-Melech, the officer who was in the court; and he burned the chariots of the sun with fire" (2 Kings 23: 11, emphasis mine). In this case King Josiah dealt with two kinds of mascots—horses and chariots.

Let us emphasize that horses and chariots in themselves are not offensive, but not when they are used as satanic mascots. Notice that King Josiah dealt with the horses and chariots because of their link with the worship of the sun—a practice God condemns vehemently. "And take heed, lest you lift your eyes to heaven, and when you see the sun, the moon, and the stars, all the host of heaven, you feel driven to worship them and serve them, which the LORD your God has given to all the people under the whole heaven as a heritage" (Deut. 4: 19).

Please also notice that the enemies of God strategically positioned these dedicated horses "at the entrance to the house of the LORD," to counter the worship of the true God.

In these last days, God wants the church to wage war with knowledge. Notice that the symbols of such dedicated horses and chariots would have similar effects as the mascots they represent. All over our cities, institutions, industries and even in our churches are mascots and symbols that establish dedication to Satan. Some monuments that 'beautify' round-abouts, road-junctions and public buildings and parks are satanic mascots and symbols. We must do prayer warfare against these mascots and symbols and pressurize government and private agencies to remove them for destruction in line with the word of God in Deuteronomy 7:5; "But thus you shall deal with them; you shall destroy their altars, and break down their sacred pillars, and cut down their wooden images, and burn their carved images with fire".

Please also notice that God was angry with what He called "wicked abominations"—which were actually symbols and drawings of certain animals, connected with satanism, as well as the symbols of idols, "portrayed all around on the walls" (see Ezekiel 8:9-10). You can now understand why some religions, occultic societies, spiritualists and native doctors use symbols like the moon and star, pharaoh's head, cobra or python, mermaid, syanks, etc. God is offended with the drawings He calls "wicked abominations" because He knows what they stand for. They are satanic symbols.

I accept that the major challenge in this kind of strategic warfare is the ability to recognize the mascots or symbols for what they really stand for —especially when what are ordinarily harmless objects or animals are used. This is where the practice of spiritual mapping and spiritual discernment come in. (Please see the chapter on 'Spiritual mapping' in my book *Waging War*

With Knowledge). The existence of satanic mascots and symbols would prove our undoing in spiritual warfare, unless we repent of their existence and destroy them. I encourage you to critically examine the mascots, symbols, logo and trade marks of public and private institutions like those in-charge of the Ports, Public Electricity supply, the Oil Companies, FESTAC, etc., you will begin to understand why we are too vulnerable to Satan in this country.

12

MYSTERY OF SYMBOLIC GESTURES

S ymbolic gestures and actions are gestures and actions that have deeper meanings and implications than what the gestures/actions portray. Satan is known to use these symbolic gestures and actions to perpetuate his wickedness. At a time the meaning and implication of such symbolic gestures and actions were fully understood by those who initiated them, but later on their full meaning/spiritual implications may be lost or shrouded in secrecy.

God and His people started the use of symbolic gestures/ actions before it was copied and perverted by Satan and his followers. For instance, circumcision of male children is a symbolic gesture which finds meaning in the covenant God instituted with Abraham and his descendants: "And God said to Abraham; 'as for you, you shall keep my covenant, you and your descendants after you throughout their generations. This is my covenant which you shall keep, between me and you and your descendants after you; every male child among you shall be circumcised" (Gen. 17:9-10).

You will also notice a couple of symbolic actions in Genesis 17:7-18, which depict the establishment of a covenant between God and Abraham. People have also done some symbolic actions in the name of traditional marriage rites, chieftaincy rites, burial rites, cloth-tying ceremonies and in some social functions which, known or unknown to them have initiated them into the occult or established a covenant with Satan! Ignorance is no excuse—see Leviticus 5: 17.

Notice that the setting aside of seven ewes by Abraham in his dealing with Abimelech was a symbolic gesture to secure the ownership of the well (see Gen. 21:28-30). Some occult men are known to have given gifts to unsuspecting people by which they establish control over the people or lay claim over their property or finances. Some occultic 'philanthropists' are known to prepare annual feasts for their village people with cows, which had their eyes plucked off and the tongues cut off. This is a satanic symbolic action, which allows the 'philanthropist' to continue to exploit the villagers while they remain <u>blind</u> and <u>mute</u> to his wicked actions.

It was also reported at intercessory circles that a particular military head of state imported into this country, one thousand blind mice with their little mouths locked with tiny padlocks. This was a satanic symbolic action to keep Nigerians <u>blind</u> and <u>mute</u> so that he could continue to have his way—but our God dealt with him!!!

Prayer exercise 1

"Father I repent of spiritual blindness which has made me and the rest of the church ignorant, and have therefore become victims of satanic spells and manipulations. By the power in the blood of Jesus Christ I break this spell and I command the eyes of your people to open in the name of Jesus. Father frustrate the tokens of wicked men and drive diviners mad in Jesus' mighty name" (Based on Isa. 42: 18-20, Isa. 44: 25).

As a positive symbolic action Abraham planted a tree in Beersheba. But what he did was actually more than planting a tree—he raised an altar to God Almighty. "Then Abraham planted a tamarisk tree in Beersheba, and there called on the name of the LORD, the Everlasting God" (Gen. 21:33). From this scripture, symbolic tree planting in government protocol can have deep spiritual implications. This is why we are worried concerning the fact that Murmur Gadaffi did a symbolic tree planting in Kano (northern Nigeria) few years ago. It is clear that people can plant trees, or other things, to establish satanic control in a place.

Prayer exercise 2

"I declare that every tree that my Father has not planted, or which has not been planted to glorify God Almighty, be uprooted in Jesus name". (Based on Matt. 15: 13).

13

ACCURSED THINGS

Accursed things are things which have become abominable by virtue of their direct involvement in satanism, idol worship, occultism, spiritism, etc; or by virtue of a curse pronounced by God or Satan. They become tools in the hands of the devil because when they are present in the homes, offices, businesses and churches of the people of God they attract destruction. Accursed things include idols and their replica, syanks and occultic crosses, 'ofor' (Ibo) or satanic staff of office, charms, occult rings and books, scapular, chaplets and talisman, etc. "You shall burn the carved images of their gods with fire; you shall not covet the silver or gold that is on them, nor take it for yourselves, lest you be snared by it; for it is an abomination to the LORD your God. Nor shall you bring an abomination into your house, lest you be doomed to destruction like it. You shall utterly detest it and utterly abhor it, for it is AN ACCURSED THING" (Deut. 7: 25-26, emphasis mine).

This scripture is a stern warning to the people of God. Such accursed things must be destroyed and burnt no matter their value—even the silver and gold attached to them must be abhorred and destroyed! Notice that such accursed things of great value were destroyed after people's conversion in Acts 19:19. "Also, many of those who had practiced magic brought their books together and burned them in the sight of all. And they counted up the value of them, and it totaled fifty thousand pieces of silver." (Fifty thousand pieces of silver must have been a lot of money then, considering that Jesus Christ was sold, few years before, for thirty pieces of silver).

In the story of Joshua the people of God lost a battle because of the presence of accursed things in the camp of God's people. The issue of accursed things is so serious that their presence in Achan's tent had an evil consequence in the whole camp of God's people. The consequences of the presence of an accursed thing in a place are far-reaching. In response to Joshua's frustration over loosing the battle of Ai God said important things we need to understand regarding accursed things. "Therefore the children of Israel could not stand before their enemies, but turned their backs before their enemies, because they have become doomed to destruction. <u>Neither will I be with you anymore</u>, unless you destroy the accursed from among you" (Josh. 7:12, emphasis mine).

The presence of accursed things nullified the promise of God to Joshua (in Joshua 1:5). "No man shall be able to stand before you all the days of your life; as I was with Moses, so I will be with you. I will not leave you nor forsake you". In other words, no matter how much you pray; and no matter the promises of God to you, you are doomed to failure when an accursed thing is present!! The mere presence of an accursed thing attracts failure and destruction to a person or place. I believe that this is one of the reasons God specified that helping to discern accursed things should be one of the duties of priest. "And they shall teach my people the difference between the holy and the unholy, and cause them to discern between the unclean and the clean" (Ezek. 44:23).

The thing to do is to first rid an environment of accursed things before prosecuting warfare against the kingdom of darkness. One of Satan's wiles is to blind the eyes of people from recognizing the accursed things for what they really are. He also encourages believers to despise and disregard accursed things as inconsequential. The height of Satan's success in this is that some believers and Churches even proudly display accursed things as souvenirs and decorations!!!

Prayer exercise

"Open my eyes O Lord to be able to identify all accursed things in my environment. Give me grace to abhor them no matter what their value is and to completely destroy them by fire. I silence every speakings of accursed things by the blood of Jesus and I command the fire of the Holy Ghost to burn them, in Jesus mighty name" (Based on Deut. 7: 25-26).

14

SATANIC ALTARS AND SHRINES

S atanic altars and shrines establish a satanic aura or
spell over a place. Their presence tends to impose
'darkness' over a place in the spirit realm. The area
under their influence is more prone to Satan's rule
or demonic infiltration unless countered by effective
prayer warfare.

The extent of the area that comes under satanic
influence due to the existence of altars, shrines or idols
depends on their power, which often depends on the
nature and regularity of sacrifices made in such places.
For instance, sacrifices that involve human beings or
human blood would produce more satanic power and
influence than sacrifices that involve just food items
or animals. This is why Satan has encouraged many
so-called 'traditional' practices, which are actually
idolatrous and demonic practices in our communities
so that more satanic altars are raised.

Satan's manipulation in this regard could be so strong as
to get even the people of God to associate with or even

join in idolatry as recorded in Psalm 106: 35-38; "But they mingled with the gentiles and learned their works; they served their idols which became a snare to them. They even sacrificed their sons and their daughters to demons, and shed innocent blood, the blood of their sons and daughters, whom they sacrificed to the idols of Canaan; and the land was polluted with blood."

Apart from establishing satanic influence and demonic infiltration, the presence of satanic altars, shrines or idols attracts the judgment of God to a place; "Therefore the wrath of the LORD was kindled against His people, so that He abhorred His own inheritance. And He gave them into the hand of the Gentiles, and those who hated them ruled over them" (Ps. 106: 40-41). With the above understanding it becomes easy to appreciate why we must not rest until all satanic altars, idols and shrines around us are destroyed. Their presence would have negative effects on us even though we are not involved in their idolatry. Gideon was not involved in his father's idolatry yet God commanded him to first destroy his father's idol before responding to God's call. Many believers and Churches are manipulated from satanic altars, shrines or prayer houses around them! Some are tied at such satanic altars or have their blessings tied at such altars.

Dealing with satanic altars, shrines, idolatry and religious pervasion must include the aggressive propagation of the gospel of Jesus Christ so that people could turn from their evil practices to stop polluting the environment. The action would include prayer warfare against the satanic altars, idols and the idolaters. "Then your altars shall be desolate, your incense altars shall be broken and I will cast down your slain men before your idols" (Ezek. 6: 4). You may also use Jeremiah 10:11, 14-15 to pray.

However, prayer warfare should not be a substitute for physical destruction and burning with fire, when the satanic altars, shrines, idols and satanic artifacts are within our reach. "But thus you shall deal with them: you shall destroy their altars and break down their sacred pillars, and cut down their wooden images, and burn their carved images with fire" (Deut. 7:5). See also Deuteronomy 12:1-4. The things that cannot burn, like metals, should be passed through fire before being disposed off. It is therefore wrong to merely pack these things and dump them in a bush or river without burning. It is also wrong to return these satanic artifacts to the satanic priests or cults. This shall only be a mere transfer of the satanic altars and artifacts. One could still be manipulated or influenced by these satanic artifacts from their new locations.

If you have made the mistake of throwing the offensive things away or returning them to satanic people, without burning, you may pray the following prayers.

Prayer exercise 1

'Father, I repent for not obeying your command to destroy and burn satanic artifacts. Lord forgive me and cleanse me with the blood of Jesus.

I separate myself and my family from these artifacts, and I break any influence or manipulation over us by the blood of Jesus. I call down the fire of the Holy Ghost upon these artifacts wherever they may be now in Jesus name. I arrest any demons that come from them, and set them on fire in Jesus name. I ask, dear Lord, that you frustrate the token of liars and drive any diviners who may use them against me mad in Jesus mighty name'. (Based on Deut. 7:5, 1 John 1:7, Jer. 5:14, Isa. 44:25).

However, it is necessary to mention that destruction and burning with fire may not necessarily be the end of every thing satanic in a shrine, grove or site of idol. God has often revealed invisible altars still standing in the spirit realm at the former sites of idols or shrines that were cut down and burnt with fire. We were praying in the house of one minister whose family suffered from constant satanic oppression when God gave us a vision. The Lord showed an altar seen as a branched palm tree standing and speaking in the beautiful sitting room of the family. The Lord explained that the house was built on the site of a former shrine.

To complete the destruction of satanic altars, shrines or idols we need to pray this prayer after the physical destruction and burning with fire.

Prayer exercise 2

"Father, I bring repentance for the idolatry, occultism and religious pervasion practiced in this place. Lord

forgive the fact that satanic altars were raised here to provoke you to anger. Lord have mercy.

You remaining satanic altars in this place—I prophesy against you to become desolate and be broken in pieces in the name of Jesus. I dry up the satanic oil that has sustained your existence. Let the earthquake of the Lord uproot any remaining satanic altars, in Jesus name.

I reconcile you land to God by the blood of Jesus. I hereby raise an altar to God with oil—in the name of the Father, the Son and the Holy Spirit, Amen!!" (Based on 1John 1:9, Ezek. 6:4, Isa. 29:6, Col. 1:20 and Gen. 28:18-19).

You may follow-up by proclaiming an appropriate scripture like Revelation chapter 5, to establish the lord-ship of Christ in the place formerly under Satan's control.

Please note that heart-felt identificational repentance (repenting for the sins of others on their behalf) breaks the legal grounds of Satan to continue to occupy a place. This 'softens' the ground to finally deal with the invisible altars. If proper repentance is not done initially, the prayer warfare may fail or may only be partially successful.

15

BURIED CHARMS AND SATANIC OBJECTS

Buried charms and satanic objects are door-openers. They open doors for demonic infestation in a place. They also produce a satanic aura over their area of influence depending on their satanic powers.

The same approach and reasoning should be followed as in dealing with satanic altars and shrines (as in No. 12 above). Sometimes the Lord may reveal the exact spot where the thing is buried and may lead one to dig it up. I was once led to dig up a ram's head in the compound of an elder in a pentecostal church. Out of fear for his safety and that of his family during a chieftaincy tussle he consulted a false prophet. This false prophet came and did ministrations in his compound, leading to the burying of the ram's head and an earthen pot at the gate of the compound.

Sometimes it may not be necessary, or even practicable, to begin to dig around a compound looking for charms and satanic objects. Some may be inaccessible under houses. In such a case, prophetic prayers should be used to deal with the buried charms and satanic objects. Appropriate weapons of God should be used to destroy or excavate the charms/satanic objects in the spirit realm. (Sometimes the Lord answers this prayer by physically digging up and exposing the offending objects on the surface using lightening, flood or wind). The land may also be commanded to vomit, eat up or swallow the charms or satanic objects.

Prayer exercise

"Father I bring repentance for the existence of charms and satanic objects in this place. I command the earthquake, lightening and fire of God to destroy them in the name of Jesus Christ. I command the land to swallow them up forever, in Jesus name. I ask that a mighty flood of the blood of Jesus should carry away all traces of charms and satanic objects here. I reconcile this land to God by the blood of Jesus" (Based on 1 John 1:9, Isa.29: 6, Num. 16:31-33, Col. 1:20).

16

ACCURSED LAND AND EVIL

FORESTS

Land can become accursed by virtue of idolatrous, occultic or demonic activities to which the land has been subjected to in the past or present. Land can also be accursed by virtue of judgment pronounced by God or a servant of God on a particular parcel of land. For instance, because of the pronouncements made by Joshua over Jericho, it became an accursed land.

"Then Joshua charged them at that time, saying, cursed be the man before the Lord who rises up and builds this city Jericho; he shall lay its foundation with his firstborn, and with his youngest he shall set up its gates" (Josh. 6:26).

A place can become an evil forest when it is formally devoted to Satan by those who have legal right over the parcel of land. In the past, certain virulent altars were raised to Satan there, and the bodies of people who died of strange diseases or under abominable conditions were thrown in there. Satan is very legalistic and would try to keep up his control over accursed lands or evil forests, even after modernization has caught up with such parcels of land. He will cast a cover of darkness over such parcels of land and would try to exert his influence over adjoining parcels of land and people living on, or living close to such parcels of land. If such portions of land are not redeemed and the curses over them broken, the effects of the curses and evil altars will remain for 100's of years.

Notice that the curses Joshua pronounced on Jericho (in Joshua 6:26) devastated an innocent, but ignorant family, about 500 years later, in I Kings16: 34.

"In his days Hiel of Bethel built Jericho. He laid its foundation with Abiran his firstborn, and with his youngest son Segub he set up its gates, <u>according to the word of the LORD, which he had spoken through Joshua the son of Nun</u>".

Also, please observe that the effect of the curse lasted for many more years until broken by Prophet Elisha in 2 Kings 2:20-22. Please notice that some of the effects of the curse on Jericho were that the water was bad and the land barren (2King 2:19). 'Bad water' and 'barren land' could impose diseases and imitations on the inhabitants of a land. This is how many people—including Christians and churches—are ignorantly suffering because of the spiritual condition of their land or compound. Such parcels of land or compounds that have become defiled by sin and unrighteousness, in addition, vomit their inhabitants. "For the land is defiled; therefore I visit the punishment of its iniquity upon it, and the land vomits out its inhabitants" (Lev.18: 25).

The stress, strain, crisis, business failure, breakdown of vehicles/machinery, break-up of marriages, financial distress, etc, experienced in some compounds or parcels of land may be manifestations of the land vomiting its inhabitants. If land redemption or land deliverance ministration is not done, the unpleasant effects may continue for a long time and serve the purpose of Satan.

The process of dealing such land include:

1. Doing spiritual mapping to reveal what went wrong in the past. (Please see my book: *Waging War with Knowledge*, for details of Spiritual Mapping).
2. Doing identificational repentance (with fasting)—addressing the specific sins as much as possible.
3. Dealing with the satanic altars on the land as described earlier.
4. Judging the demons and principalities on the land.
5. Lifting curses from the land.
6. Reconciling the land to God by the blood of Jesus.
7. Raising an altar to God and anointing it with oil.
8. Pronouncing blessings upon the land.

These eight steps are the necessary steps for dedicating a land/compound to God.

17

SATANIC PLANTINGS

In the course of doing family, land or territorial deliverance God sometimes pointed out to us ornamental plants, shrubs or trees that must be physically uprooted because of satanic connections. Sometimes it is not clear how they became satanic since some of them were planted by the Christian families themselves. In some cases, God revealed that the cuttings or seedlings came from satanic plants/trees. The trees or shrubs you planted could mean that you have established an offshoot from satanic trees/shrines. This often applies to common trees/shrines like 'Oha', 'Ogirishi' and 'Ngwu' (in Igbo language). It is therefore advisable to pray over and redeem cuttings and seedlings from the hands of the devil, before planting.

Sometimes, when the Lord implicates such trees, shrubs and ornamental plants, He may ask you to pray over them, may be anointing with oil. But He may also ask you to uproot and destroy. You should obey promptly no matter how valuable the tree/shrub is to you.

However in some of our operations, God has revealed 'satanic plantings' in a vision. Such 'plantings' are invisible satanic devices used by Satan to extend his area of influence over a territory, or used as a booster station for his diabolic purposes. Sometimes the Lord reveals these invisible 'satanic plantings' as flowers, shrubs, christmas trees or other uncharacterized structures in the environment or even inside a house.

Some 'satanic plantings' are also placed demonically inside people's body to cause sickness. These may be planted in the head, breast, stomach, limbs, womb or private part of a woman. These 'plantings' sometimes 'move' or 'grow' in the places where they are planted. Few days ago a lady I counselled with told me that she felt that a male organ was planted in her private part. She felt a sensation of someone having sex with her while she was walking in broad daylight—without seeing the person.

Dealing with 'satanic plantings' would therefore vary depending on whether they are visible or invisible or whether they are in the environment or within someone's body. However it would usually involve anointing with oil, laying on of hands, accompanied with violent prayers.

Prayer exercise

"Father I command the wind to blow and uproot every satanic plantings—visible and invisible—in Jesus name. Every plant my father has not planted should be uprooted.

I curse your roots to dry up. I curse you to shrivel and die in the name of Jesus. Let the fire of the Holy Ghost completely burn you up in Jesus name. I speak forth healing and restoration where damage has been caused in Jesus mighty name Amen"(Based on Jer. 49:36, Matt. 15:13, Job 22:28, Jer. 5:14, Jer. 30:17).

When such prayers are prayed with sufficient faith some implicated physical trees or shrubs die or fall. [You may please see chapter 11 of my book; *Waging War With Knowledge*, International Edition, for full testimonies of a satanic tree that was uprooted physically, through prayer judgment].

18

MISUSE OF UMBILICAL STUMP, PLACENTA AND BABY'S HAIR

In the name of tradition Satan taught our fathers to unwittingly open their children to demonic control and manipulation. In many cultures, especially in Africa, umbilical stump, placenta and a baby's first crop of hair barbed are treated in a ritualistic way.

The umbilical stump that falls off the navel of a new-born baby is planted in the soil at the root of a chosen plant like coconut, palm tree, plantain, etc. When such trees, begin to fruit, the babies (now grown up), whose umbilical stumps were planted with the trees become the 'sole owners' of such trees and their fruits. Such children become identified with the trees in whose roots their umbilical stumps were buried.

The mystery that Satan takes advantage of is that the navel is a spiritual gate. Through the umbilical cord attached to the navel, the baby received oxygen, blood, nutrients and hereditary factors from the mother, while the baby was in the womb. Burying the umbilical stump ritualistically, opens up the child (or full-grown adult) to demonic transfer and control through the umbilical gate. The tree at whose root the umbilical stump was 'planted' stands as an 'altar' which speaks into

the life of the individual. Relationship between the tree and the individual becomes so close that the state of health of such tree may determine the state of health of the individual. This is a kind of strange 'soul-tie' between a tree and a person! A premature death of such a tree could mean a pre-mature physical death of the concerned individual. That is why sudden death, or major afflictions, could come upon somebody who goes to cut down such a tree linked with his or her life, while manifesting zeal without knowledge.

In some cultures, the placenta that comes out following the delivery of a baby is treated in similar ritualistic ways. Sometimes the placenta is lodged with water spirits in the river opening the child to manipulation or control from water-spirits.

In some cultures also, the first crop of hair cut off from a baby's head—usually when the child is one year old—is also treated in similar ritualistic ways. In such cases the head of the child, which is important spiritually to receive the laying of hands or the anointing oil of God, becomes open to demonic interferences.

While the mystery of satanic enslavement can not be explained fully in all cases, one should understand that a people would play into the hands of Satan when they transgress the commandment of God, like that in Leviticus18: 30.

"Therefore you shall keep my ordinance, so that you do not commit any of these ABOMINABLE CUSTOMS which were committed before you, and that you do not DEFILE YOURSELVES by them: I am the LORD your God" (emphasis mine).

Dealing with this trick of Satan would include enlightening our people, especially those in the rural areas, about the far-reaching spiritual implications of these ABOMINABLE CUSTOMS. People often ask the question about how this part of the body should be rightly disposed of. I suggest that one should pray over them, covering them with the blood of Jesus, to prevent them getting into wrong hands. Then they can be disposed off in a non-ritualistic way in the toilet system or by ordinary burying.

The prayer below is a model that could be employed by one whose umbilical cord was 'planted' at the root of a tree. The prayer will be more effective with fasting, by the side of (or while laying hand on) the implicated tree, if the tree is known.

Prayer exercise

"Father, I repent of this and other abominable customs of my people. I bring repentance that I was dedicated to Satan through the 'planting' of my umbilical stump (placenta or hair).I separate my life and destiny from the remaining traces of what was planted! I separate

my life and destiny from the satanic altar so raised, and from the life of this tree. I curse the satanic altar to dry up and become desolate in Jesus name. I silence any further speaking from this altar into my life by the blood of Jesus. I curse this tree to shrivel and die, in the mighty name of Jesus Christ." (Based on I John 1:9, Lev.18: 30, Heb12: 24, Job.22: 28)

It is even better that this deliverance ministration is done on one's behalf by an anointed servant of God at the base of the implicated tree, or as close to the Land as possible. This prayer ministration may be followed by the cutting down of the relevant tree because of the pervasion it was subjected to. We must warn that such a tree must not be cut down before the issues of the victim's life has been properly separated from the tree.

19

MONITORING GADGETS

A s the name implies, Satan uses certain gadgets to
eavesdrop, observe or spy on Christians' churches
or programmes. Sometimes the Holy Spirit gives visions
and/or dreams to reveal which gadget(s) are implicated.
These satanic gadgets include satanic 'eyes,' 'ears',
cameras, recording equipment, computers, antenna,
satellite dish, telephone and other telecommunication
systems.

I recall an incidence in Oleh, Delta State, when a
confessing witch told of how they monitored the words
I spoke in a church from a house in the village.

Even when the Holy Spirit does not reveal, I suggest
that specifically dealing with satanic monitoring
gadgets should be a normal feature of our prayers, or
in doing opening prayers for a programme or a prayer
session. Sometimes the 'eyes' and 'ears' of the enemy
are hidden in the normal objects in the room. This
strategy is often used against those who have grown in
relevance to the Kingdom of God or who are a terror to

the kingdom of Satan. I remember when God revealed an 'eye' in a globe (map of the world) in my office, from where the enemy tried to monitor me and our activities.

Prayer exercise

"I blind the peeping 'eyes' of the enemy with hot arrows of fire. I smash the listening 'ear' of the enemy with the sledgehammer of the Holy Ghost.

I lift up the sword of the Lord and I cut in pieces every satanic monitoring gadget and the telecommunication system of the enemy. I jam their listening devices and I set their control rooms in the air, on the land and in the waters on fire, in the name of Jesus Christ. I throw a giant dragnet of the Holy Ghost and I catch all the demonic spies and destroy them with fire in Jesus mighty name." (Based on 2 Kings 13:17, Jer.23: 29, Ezek.21: 9-10, Jer5: 14, Ezek.17: 20).

20

SATANIC BOOSTER STATIONS

In telecommunications, booster stations boost or intensify electronic signals in a place, to increase the impact of a distant or remote transmission house. Satan also employs this principle to extend his influence over a place.

Objects of varying nature, with or without direct contact with the occult, could serve the kingdom of darkness as booster stations. Practical examples would explain this satanic device better.

My team and I were ministering in the comfortable home of a Christian family when the Holy Spirit gave us an eye-opining revelation. The Lord showed that the locally made strip of carpet was made from snake skin. The Holy Sprit said that the enemy was using that material as a booster station for the snake worship in the village of the man. This ministration came in the Port Harcourt home of a man whose village of nativity is at least nine hours journey away in the western part of Nigeria. It was easy for me to observe that the family was a bit skeptical concerning this revelation when it was shared.

Some time later we traveled to the village of this man to deal with evil foundations in their ancestral root. In our presence, the man in question asked his father concerning the matter of snake worship. The old man confirmed that his own late father kept a sacred snake in a water container. He told us that this sacred water was applied to people's body to procure healing. This old man then reminded his son, our host, that he also benefited from such ministration with the snake water when he was sick as a child. This confirmed the existence of an altar of snake worship in the village, for which Satan used the expensive snake skin material as booster station miles away in Port Harcourt, to continue to oppress the family.

Satan can also use natural, moulded or carved tortoise shell, fish, lion, and elephant, etc. as booster stations to extend the influence of the ancestral guiding spirits far from the land of nativity. Some ancestral families had guiding spirits that manifested as certain beasts. We once ministered in a Port Harcourt home where God revealed that the remotely located ancestral guiding spirit was networking with the idolatrous features of the family's immediate environment, to extend its influence on the family.

In one particular year my mother came under attack by the spirit of death. The Lord revealed that the spirit of death was programmed into her sitting room via a picture of a river in a calendar on her wall. In that case an ordinary picture of a river on a calendar became a booster station for an attack from the water kingdom.

I was present in a meeting when a deliverance minister shared the story of how his wife nearly died following an attack launched against her through the picture of 'Jesus' hanging in the sitting room. Following a revelation of giant flies covering the picture in the spirit realm the picture was pulled down and set on fire. This brought about some demonic manifestations in the woman before she was finally delivered.

In this last example, a legal ground was created for Satan by hanging a picture of 'Jesus.' Remember that first of all there was no photography when Jesus walked on earth, so nobody took a picture of him. So all the pictures purported as 'JESUS' border on falsehood which is Satan's main territory. Secondly the Bible says clearly in Exodus 20:4: "You shall not make for yourself a carved image—any likeness of any thing that is in heaven above . . . ." Wherever scripture is broken a territory has been created for Satan! Pictures, sculptures, and carvings of 'Jesus'; 'Mary', angels, etc may spell trouble for homes, offices or Churches where they are kept!

How do we then deal with this kind of satanic device? First of all we need to pray over and dedicate to God, everything we buy or bring into our homes, offices and churches—even ball-point pens. Remember that the occult group, which calls itself a church, that is based in calabar, Nigeria, massively distributed ball-point pens at a time. They may have used these pens as points of contact or booster stations in homes, offices, churches, etc. Secondly, stay away from things or objects that are directly or indirectly connected to the occult, or that carry occultic symbols. Such occultic symbols may be drawing of snakes, half-moon and stars, syanks, signs of the zodiac, etc. Thirdly, bring repentance for the existence of things in your possession which may be booster stations for the kingdom of darkness. Fourthly ask the Holy Spirit for discernment to be able to identify the things around you which can serve the purposes of Satan. Sought them out and physically destroy by fire—see Deuteronomy 12:1-5. Fifthly, clear the home, office, premises of all demonic presence, attracted by such satanic booster stations. Finally sanctify the place afresh by pleading the blood of Jesus and anointing with oil. "Then Moses took the anointing oil, and anointed the tabernacle and all that was in it, and consecrated them" (Lev.8: 10).

Prayer exercise

"Father, I bring repentance for the existence of satanic booster stations in my home. I ask that you please grant me discernment to spot them and destroy them. Even now I release the fire of the Holy Ghost to burn them. I disconnect every object, picture, souvenir, etc., in this place from the kingdom of darkness. I establish a wall of fire right round my home to screen off any satanic projection unto any object in my home

I set fire on Satan's transmission stations in the heavens, in the air, in the water and on the land, in Jesus name. I arrest the demons involved in supervising these evil transmissions, in Jesus name. I cover every object in my home with the blood of Jesus. I re-sanctify my home for the indwelling of the Holy Spirit with this anointing oil, in Jesus mighty name, Amen" (Based on Lev.5: 17, Jer.5: 14, Lev.8: 10-11).

21

MIND ASSAULT

When a person is born again, God expects him to renew his mind. "And do not be conformed to this world, but be transformed by the renewing of your mind, that you may prove what is that good and acceptable and perfect will of God" (Rom.12: 2). The essence of renewing the mind is for the believer to strive to discover and conform to the perfect will of God in all things.

Often times Satan assaults the mind of the believer with suggestions and manipulations that encourages the believer to remain in the previous mind-set before regeneration. Satan also assaults the believer's mind to accept suggestions, positions and compromises that are not in line with the perfect will of God.

Sometimes demons cast thoughts on the mind of a believer—thoughts which do not originate from the believer. Such thoughts may be outrageous—like thoughts to kill another person or thoughts to commit rape or a solicitation towards evil. Satan would turn around to accuse the believer as if such thoughts originated from him. Some believers have felt guilty, ashamed and condemned for thoughts that were not their own, but projected into their minds by demons. In such a state the believer is neutralized and can no more do effective prayer warfare against Satan's kingdom. Moreover, self-condemnation could lead to self-pity and depression. Such a believer may thereby open the doorway for demonic oppression.

It is our responsibility to shut our minds against ungodly thoughts or evil thoughts projected by demons. The bible admonishes us; "keep your heart with all diligence, for out of it spring the issues of life" (Prov. 4: 23).

Sometimes, Satan's assault against the believer's mind is in the form of projecting condemnation over a sin, or sins, one has confessed and obtained forgiveness from God. In such a case it will help us to remember that when a person confesses and forsakes his sins "none of the transgressions which he has committed shall be remembered against him . . ." (Ezek. 18:22). God will totally forget the sin. The bible says; that "whoever confesses and forsakes them (sins) will have mercy" (Prov. 28:13). One should actively appropriate the forgiveness and mercy of God. One should also promptly forgive one's self. One should therefore reject the condemnation that is motivated by Satan!

Prayer exercise

"Father, I thank you because you have not observed iniquity in me. Thank you because I am free from conde-mnation.

I plead the blood of Jesus on my heart and mind to blot out every evil thought. I garrison my heart with the blood of Jesus to protect my heart from demon-projected thoughts in Jesus name. I come against you demons that project evil and defeatist thoughts into my mind in Jesus name. Let the fire of the Holy Ghost roast you in Jesus mighty name, Amen" (Based on Num.23: 21, Rom. 8:1, Prov. 4:23, Jer. 5: 14).

Books by Evangelist Onyechi Daniel.

1. *Waging War With Knowledge, doing strategic spiritual warfare and bold intercession.*
2. *War A Good Warfare.*
3. *Partnership, Teamwork and Networking in spiritual warfare.*
4. *Exposing Satanic Devices—doing targeted prayerwarfare.*

Information about the author

Onyechi Daniel was called by God as an evangelist and teacher. He is quite involved in the prophetic and apostolic moves of God and in the prayer movements that cut across denominational boundaries. He is involved in stirring ministers towards unity and networking.

The Lord had led him consistently, deeper and deeper into the fields of spiritual warfare and intercession. He is a pharmacist turned preacher. He is the president of Power House Ministries Int'l, a non-denominational ministry based in Port Harcourt, Nigeria. He can be reached through:

Power House Ministries Int'l,

12 First Avenue, (opp. 28 Rumuibekwe Rd.),
P.O.Box 9682,
Port Harcourt,
Nigeria.
E-mail: oudaniel2000@yahoo.com:
Tel: (234)-84-480240.

CPSIA information can be obtained at www.ICGtesting.com
Printed in the USA
LVOW08s1601160815

450320LV00001B/16/P